G000135408

Published by
Lion Publishing plc
Sandy Lane West,
Oxford, England
www.lion-publishing.co.uk
ISBN 0 7459 4223 7
First edition 2000
10 9 8 7 6 5 4 3 2 1 0
A catalogue record for this
book is available from the
British Library
Typeset in 11/15
Elegant Garamond
Printed and bound in Singapore

Acknowledgments

12, 60: Song of Songs 8:10,
I Corinthians 13:8, 13,
quoted from the Good News
Bible published by The Bible
Societies/HarperCollins
Publishers Ltd, UK © American
Bible Society 1966, 1971, 1976,
1992, used with permission.
55: Song of Songs 8:7,
quoted from The New Revised
Standard Version of the Bible,
Anglicized Edition, copyright
© 1989, 1995 by the Division
of Christian Education of
the National Council of the
Churches of Christ in the
United States of America, and
used by permission. All rights
reserved. Every effort has been
made to trace and acknowledge
copyright holders of all the
quotations in this book. We
apologize for any errors or
omissions that may remain, and
would ask those concerned to
contact the publishers, who will
ensure that full acknowledgment
is made in the future.

Happy anniversary

Compiled by Sarah Hall

LION
Giftlines

Take time together

It's your anniversary. The wedding
day goes by in a blur of
excitement and you find
yourselves launched into
the adventure of marriage.
Amid the rush, there is little time
to reflect.

Yet as a character in one of C.S. Lewis's books remarks, 'A pleasure is full grown when it is remembered.' An anniversary can be a special opportunity to pause and to take stock of the achievements of the years. It is a time set aside for you to remember the problems overcome, the joys experienced, and to give thanks for the uniqueness of your love.

For Better ...

*I*n the opinion of the world, marriage ends all, as it does in a comedy. The truth is precisely the opposite: it begins all.

ANNE SOPHIE SWETCHINE

N o, I haven't any formula. I can just say it's been a very happy experience… a successful marriage I think gets happier as the years go by, that's about all.

Dwight D. Eisenhower

M

*y lover knows that with him
I find contentment and peace.*

FROM THE OLD TESTAMENT SONG OF SONGS

I would like to go through life side by side with you, telling you more and more until we grew to be one being together until the hour should come for us to die.

JAMES JOYCE

Oh the comfort, the inexpressible comfort of feeling safe with a person, having neither to weigh thoughts nor measure words, but pouring them all right out, just as they are, chaff and grain together; certain that a faithful hand will take and sift them, keep what is worth keeping, and then with the breath of kindness throw the rest away.

DINAH MARIA MULOCK CRAIK

M*arried couples who love each other tell each other a thousand things without talking.*

CHINESE PROVERB

I add my breath to your breath
That our days may be long
  in the earth
That the days of our people
  may be long
That we may be one person
That we may finish our roads together.

INDIAN SONG

I am your clay.
You are my clay.
In life we share a single quilt.
In death we will share one coffin.

KUAN TAO-SHENG

For Worse

L et me not to the marriage of
     true minds
Admit impediments. Love is not love
Which alters when it alteration finds,
Or bends with the remover to remove:—
O, no! it is an ever-fixèd mark
That looks on tempests, and is
     never shaken.

WILLIAM SHAKESPEARE

No man knows what the wife of his bosom is until he has gone with her through the fiery trials of this world.

WASHINGTON IRVING

L ove doesn't just sit there, like a stone, it has to be made, like bread; remade all the time, made new.

Ursula K. Le Guin

*C*hains do not hold a marriage together. It is threads, hundreds of tiny threads which sew people together through the years. That is what makes a marriage last.

SIMONE SIGNORET

We have lived and loved together
Through many changing years,
We have shared each other's gladness
And wept each other's tears.

And let us hope the future,
As the past has been will be:
I will share with thee my sorrows,
And thou thy joys with me.

CHARLES JEFFERYS

Treasure the love you receive above all. It will survive long after your gold and good health have vanished.

Og Mandino

The ring, so worn as you behold,
  So thin, so pale, is yet of gold:
The passion such it was to prove —
Worn with life's care, love yet was love.

GEORGE CRABBE

Through
Time ...

E*very day, every hour, every moment makes me feel more deeply how blessed we are in each other.*

WILLIAM WORDSWORTH

D*on't praise marriage on the third day, but after the third year.*

RUSSIAN PROVERB

So sweet love seemed that April morn,
  When first we kissed beside
  the thorn,
So strangely sweet, it was not strange
We thought that love could never change.

But I can tell – let truth be told –
That love will change in growing old;
Though day by day is nought to see,
So delicate his motions be.

ROBERT BRIDGES

L ove seems the swiftest, but it is the
slowest of all growths. No man
or woman really knows what perfect
love is until they have been married
a quarter of a century.

MARK TWAIN

W*hile unhurried days come and go,*
Let us turn to each other
in quiet affection,
walk in peace to the edge of old age.

EGYPTIAN SONG

To see a young couple loving each other is no wonder; but to see an old couple loving each other is the best sight of all.

WILLIAM MAKEPEACE THACKERAY

When marrying, one should ask oneself this question: Do you believe that you will be able to converse well with this woman into your old age?

FRIEDRICH NIETZSCHE

U*ntil you're a hundred,*
  Until I'm ninety-nine,
Together
Until white hair grows.

JAPANESE SONG

There is nothing more lovely
in life than the union of two
people whose love for one another
has grown through the years from
the small acorn of passion to a great
rooted tree. Surviving all vicissitudes,
and rich with its manifold branches,
every leaf holding its own significance.

VITA SACKVILLE-WEST

An old man
in love
is like a flower
in winter.

CHINESE PROVERB

Perfect love sometimes
does not come until
the first grandchild.

WELSH PROVERB

G row old along with me!
The best is yet to be,
The last of life, for which the first
was made.

Our times are in his hand
Who saith, 'A whole I planned,'
Youth shows but half; trust God; see all,
Nor be afraid.

ROBERT BROWNING

L ove's not Time's fool, though rosy
lips and cheeks
Within his bending sickle's compass come;
Love alters not with his brief hours
and weeks,
But bears it out ev'n to the edge of doom.

WILLIAM SHAKESPEARE

The heart has no wrinkles.

ENGLISH PROVERB

To see her is to love her,
    And love but her for ever;
For Nature made her what she is
And never made anither!

ROBERT BURNS

B*ut love me for love's sake, that
 evermore*
*Thou may'st love on through love's
 eternity.*

ELIZABETH BARRETT BROWNING

*A*ll other things, to their
destruction draw,
Only our love hath no decay;

This, no tomorrow hath, nor yesterday,
Running it never runs from us away,
But truly keeps his first, last,
   everlasting day.

JOHN DONNE

W*hat will survive of us is love.*

Philip Larkin

L ove, all alike, no season knows,
   nor clime,
Nor hours, age, months, which are
   the rags of time.

JOHN DONNE

U nable are the Loved to die
For Love is Immortality.

EMILY DICKINSON

M*any waters cannot quench love,*
neither can floods drown it.

FROM THE OLD TESTAMENT SONG OF SONGS

N o, the heart that has truly lov'd
       never forgets,
But as truly loves on to the close,
As the sunflower turns on her god, when he sets,
   when he sets,
The same look which she turn'd
   when he rose.

THOMAS MOORE

But true love is a durable fire,
  In the mind ever burning,
Never sick, never old, never dead,
From itself never turning.

SIR WALTER RALEGH

How do I love thee? Let me count the ways.
I love thee to the depth and breadth
and height
My soul can reach, when feeling
out of sight
For the end of Being and ideal Grace.

I love thee with a love I seemed to lose
With my lost saints – I love thee
with the breath,
Smiles, tears, of all my life! –
and, if God choose,
I shall but love thee better after death.

ELIZABETH BARRETT BROWNING

*L*ove is eternal. Meanwhile these three remain: faith, hope, love; and the greatest of these is love.

FROM THE NEW TESTAMENT
FIRST LETTER TO THE CORINTHIANS

As God has blessed me with your love, and you with mine, may he bless us both with his great love now and always.

AUTHOR UNKNOWN